Every Nation's Treasure: Children

Poetic Reflections

by O.K. FATAI

Published by OK Publishing

Wellington, New Zealand

Email: OK.Publishingnz@gmail.com

Full catalogue in print data may be obtained from the National Library of New Zealand

ISBN-13: 978-0-473-51138-8

Dedication

To all those who had shown that we have an inner duty to care and support children and that children is a family, society and countries future.

CONTENTS

Acknowledgements

I appreciate the help of my family and friends who value the place and roles that children play in their life journey.

seeing beauty

children are treasured
because they are blessings

to a family and to parents
children are treasured

because they are beautiful
no matter who they are

children are treasured
because they are our future

the people to carry us through
to a brighter tomorrow

and a blessed experience
when we grow old

and we see our children
we see beauties all around us.

responsibility

as adults we have responsibilities
to impart to our children

the best we can give them
for children are our greatest

responsibilities, not just
parents but a community

a country and the whole world
each one of us adults have

a responsibility to ensure
our children grow up the be

the person that fulfils their destiny
so take note of our individual responsibilities

and also of our collective responsibilities.

we only

we only receive presents and gifts
on our special days

and special events
we only receive presents and gifts

on birthdays and anniversaries
on holidays and celebrations

these gifts are not as great
as the gifts of children

yes, children are the nations
and families greatest gifts

to adore and treasure
to teach and develop

to love and take care of
for these gifts are rare diamonds

that will shine for the whole world to see.

sometimes

we sometimes see children who journey unhindered
we sometimes see children who face many obstacles

we sometimes see children who laugh all the time
we sometimes see children who cry a lot of the time

we sometimes see children who grow up to cause headache
we sometimes see children who grow up to bless the world

sometimes when children experience so much love and care
they grow so much inner strength that they become

the children that we look up to
the children that changed the world

the children that reform our lives
the children that shines like a morning star

the children that bless the whole world.

shining treasures

no matter a child's talent, still a shining treasure
no matter a child's appearance, still a shining treasure

no matter a child's religion, still a shining treasure
no matter a child's ethnicity, still a shining treasure

no matter a child's ability, still a shining treasure
no matter a child's family, still a shining treasure

no matter a child's status, still a shining treasure
no matter a child's achievements, still a shining treasure

no matter a child's education, still a shining treasure
no matter a child's background, still a shining treasure

reality is, we don't treat all our children as shining treasures
no wonder many of our children do not shine.

champions

i see the works of world vision
helping children in poverty

and distress all over the world
and when i think of all those who

gives financial help to the work
of world vision and many other

charities and organizations,
i regard those people as true champions

i regard those people as superstars
and true super people

and really they are conquerors of
today and tomorrow.

angels on earth

i may not have seen angels from heaven
i may not have dreams about angels

but i can see angels on earth
i can see dreams of angels

smiling and laughing
playing and having fun

angels that i can relate to
angels that i can talk to

angels who make me smile every day
and they are our children

the angels who can really make my day
filled with wonders and appreciations.

a gift

we have gifts we receive
in times of birthdays

and anniversaries
we have gifts to give

to friends and families
the gifts are reminders

of reaching a milestone
or achieving a goal

but there is another gift
that inspires and gives joy

it is the gifts of children
gifts to really treasure

and treat with care
for how you treat them today

can really become who they are
in the future.

butterflies

a butterflies is a gift
with beautiful colours

and amazing journey
our children are like butterflies

with transformation magic
and beauty outstanding

for when we think they
had out grown themselves

out came the butterfly
that can really bless our days.

when we treat

when we treat our children
like an angel on earth

the child will grow up
with an angelic heart

when we treat our children
like a golden treasure

or a piece of diamond
the child will grow up

shining like a piece of gold
and becomes a blessing

that the world will value
when we treat our child

with respect and adore
they will grow up

as adults who respect and
adore others

for whatever we do to our
children today

will be who they will become
in years to come.

reflections

children are like mirrors
that reflect back how

people treat them
children are like images

that reflects the words
and examples they see
daily

children are like magic
they can change and they

have tremendous amount
of resilience and fun

but deep down they
are still reflections of what

ever they experience
in their childhood years.

internalized

when we praise our children
for the good works they had done

those words of praises are internalized
when we say harsh words to our children,

those harsh words are internalized

when we say compliments to our children
that lifted their spirits and make them smile

those compliments are internalized
when we applause our children

and give them our words of approval
those words of applause are internalized

whatever we do or say to our children
whether good or bad

they are internalized in their soul
and may be seen in their behavior years later.

the wonders and magic

the beauties of children
the wonders of children

the magic of children
the miracles of children

the spectacles of children
the amazement of children

the admiration of children
the marvels of children

the sensation of children
the awe of children

they are just so divine
so treat them well

as they are from the divine.

when connect

when connect with children
connect with love and purpose

when engaged with children
engaged with grace and respect

when walking with children
do so with a spirit of care, integrity and fun

for children can know even with their young age
children can tell

and children can internalize.

auditing

we are skilled at auditing
examining how things were done

and whether we followed correct procedures and protocols
we may not know it

but children are good at auditing as well
your words, your actions, your behaviors

all observed with a careful eye
as they audit you

perhaps they may even tell you the results of your audits.

influence

you are an influence
you are a stimulus

you are a guide
you are an impact person

you are an effect
you are an inspiration

you are a motivation
you are a shaper

you are an inducer
whenever children is around you.

to build

there is a great way to build
there is an effective way to shape

there is a fantastic way to develop
there is a magical way to foster

there is an influential way to create
it is by doing everything with love

deep from the heart
from the love that comes from the very core of the soul

when you interact with children
every single time of interacting with a child.

a therapy

sometimes when things get tough
and life is harsh

it is a magical moment
to be around children

and observed the wonders of their lives
sometimes when storms meet life

being around children is like a safe have
their blessing is magical

for in tough times they can be the therapy
and source of strength we all need.

hard going

sometimes things are hard going
for many children around the world

they are the refugee children
they are the abused children

they are the children in poverty
they are the displaced children

they are the children of war
they are the children who are forced

to be soldiers
but there is always hope if the world

acted to be an anchor in their lives
to be a safe harbor

to be a fountain of real love
from which these children can drink daily from.

love that i cherish

there is a kind of love that i cherish
something that i appreciate

it's a love that children treasure
and value for the rest of their lives

it is beyond the prized value of gold
and revered by my humble soul

it is the real love given by a good loving mother
to her children.

to shape?

children should be treasured
and cherished for whoever they are

they are not there to be scolded
when they are just expressing how active they are

appreciate who they are
and cherish who they would like to become

and let the divine do the shaping and molding.

loving a child

when we love a child
we discover in our journey

amazing and wonderful places in the spirit
only discovered when we love a child

when we walk with a child
and observed the amazement of being around a child

we discover in our walk
magical rooms in the soul only opened up

when we are with a child
being with a child can produce magic

that we haven't discovered in our lives before.

sometimes we think

sometimes we think a five cents we give a child
does not matter
but it does matter

sometimes we think a small thank you we say to a child
does not matter
but it does matter

sometimes we think that a second of smile to a child
does not matter
but it does matter

when we do and say good things to a child
even how small it may be

and even when we think that they don't really matter
be aware that they do really matter.

they say it

mothers and fathers do say it
even when we don't agree with them

mothers and fathers do declare it
even when be believe otherwise

mothers and fathers do proclaim it
even when we can disagree with them

mothers and fathers do say it
that their children are just so wonderful

no matter what we think.

don't underestimate

we long to be a safe harbor for our children
during times of storm

but children can also be a safe harbor for us
sometimes we long to be a savior for our children

especially when the going gets tough
but our children can be a savior for us as well

we should never underestimate the value of children

Other books by O.K. Fatai

1. Poems on Values to Succeed Worldwide in Life: Being Responsible
2. Poems on Values to Succeed Worldwide in Life: Courage
3. Poems on Values to Succeed Worldwide in Life: Good Families
4. Poems on Values to Succeed Worldwide in Life: Forgiveness
5. Poems on Values to Succeed Worldwide in Life: Good Friends
6. Poems on Values to Succeed Worldwide in Life: Grace
7. Poems on Values to Succeed Worldwide in Life: Hope
8. Poems on Values to Succeed Worldwide in Life: Humility
9. Poems on Values to Succeed Worldwide in Life: Joy
10. Poems on Values to Succeed Worldwide in Life: Justice
11. Poems on Values to Succeed Worldwide in Life: Life
12. Poems on Values to Succeed Worldwide in Life: Love
13. Poems on Values to Succeed Worldwide in Life: Mercy
14. Poems on Values to Succeed Worldwide in Life: Peace
15. Poems on Values to Succeed Worldwide in Life: Perseverance
16. Poems on Values to Succeed Worldwide in Life: Faith
17. Poems on Values to Succeed Worldwide in Life: Harmony with Nature
18. Poems on Values to Succeed Worldwide in Life: Education

More books by O.K. Fatai

1. Poems on Values to Succeed Worldwide in Life: Understanding and Wisdom
2. Poems on Values to Succeed Worldwide in Life: Work and Optimism
3. Poems on Values to Succeed Worldwide in Life: Adversity and Confidence
4. Poems on Values to Succeed Worldwide in Life: Listening and Diversity and Unity
5. Poems on Values to Succeed Worldwide in Life: Sharing and Honesty
6. Poems on Values to Succeed Worldwide in Life: Simplicity and Harmony
7. Poems on Values to Succeed Worldwide in Life: Unity in Diversity and Connections
8. Poems on Values to Succeed Worldwide in Life: Contentment and Acceptance
9. Poems on Values to Succeed Worldwide in Life: Excellence and Compassion
10. Poems on Values to Succeed Worldwide in Life: Generosity and Being Passionate
11. Poems on Values to Succeed Worldwide in Life: Gentleness and Trustworthy
12. Poems on Values to Succeed Worldwide in Life: Patience and Being Tactful
13. Poems on Values to Succeed Worldwide in Life: Purity and Integrity
14. Poems on Values to Succeed Worldwide in Life: Being Modest and Persistence
15. Poems on Values to Succeed Worldwide in Life: Respect and Loyalty

About the Author

O.K. Fatai is a poet and author from Wellington, New Zealand. He likes to spend time writing poems, especially ones that explore the different aspects of values and virtues that are widely accepted in different cultures today.

O.K. Fatai enjoys writing songs and some of his forthcoming books are song lyrics that look at different values and virtues and some of their appeal to us today. In his spare time, he writes short stories and novels. He is looking forward to sharing these stories with readers around the world, and he has already published some short stories and has more than ten forthcoming publications in children's literature. O.K. Fatai is writing novels for young adults and adults. He is also a playwright and has written and/or directed more than eight short plays.

He likes painting abstract art and enjoys the different interpretations of abstract paintings, especially when they reflect values and virtues. He is a photographer who likes to take photographs of nature and the environment, which has a special place in his heart. He is keen on filming and editing videos, plays musical instruments and is part of a local band.

O.K. Fatai is a volunteer at the United Nations and regional prisons in Wellington and, for many years has volunteered to more than ten other organizations. He works in the health sector and is a consultant for three different online companies, and the President and CEO of more than three businesses. He is also available as an external consultant to the United Nations, the European Bank for Reconstruction and Development, and the Asian Development Bank.